WHAT IS ROUND?

by **REBECCA KAI DOTLICH**
photographs by **MARIA FERRARI**

HarperFestival®
A Division of HarperCollins*Publishers*

Tangerines, garbanzo beans,

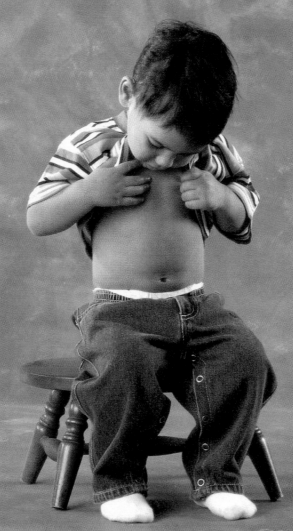

a button on a belly!

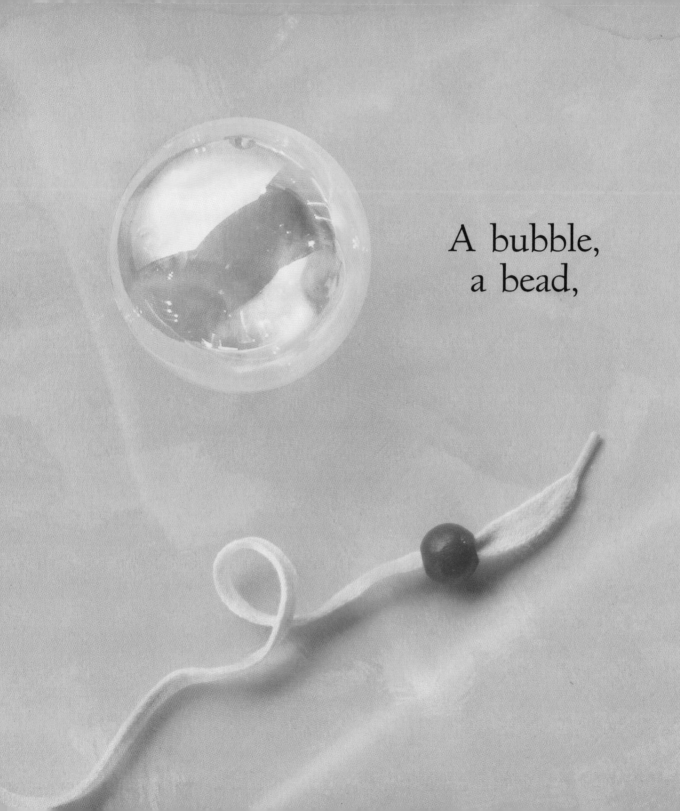

A bubble,
a bead,

a bagel,
a ball,

the lid from
a jar of jelly.

strawberry

A marble, a melon,

a nickel,

the moon!

A button, a bell,

blueberries,

balloons!

A saucer,
a circle,

a cookie, a clock,

a grape and a globe,

and sometimes a rock.

A pancake, a pea,

a penny,

a pie. . . .

What else is ROUND?